ENGLISCH LEKTÜRE

Alan Cartmell

Harry Hedgehog

für die Unterstufe

STARK

Bildnachweis:
Umschlag: Rainer Thiele

ISBN: 3-89449-444-1

D-85318 Freising · Postfach 1852 · Tel. (0 81 61) 1790

Inhalt

Autor: Alan Cartmell
Illustrator: Rainer Thiele

Vorwort

Liebe Schülerinnen, liebe Schüler,

Der Igel Harry wacht nach langem Winterschlaf auf und freut sich an den ersten Sonnenstrahlen des Frühlings. Auf seinen Erkundungsreisen durch seinen Heimatgarten und in die nähere Umgebung trifft er auf viele altbekannte aber auch auf einige neue Gesichter.
Seid ihr ein bisschen neugierig geworden?
Die Geschichte von Harrys Erlebnissen wird euch bestimmt gefallen. Sie ist in einfacher Sprache geschrieben und damit euch das Lesen leichter fällt, habe ich schwierige Wörter in der deutschen Übersetzung angegeben.

Ich wünsche euch viel Spaß beim Lesen!

Alan Cartmell

Chapter 1
Harry wakes up

If you look through the crack[1] in the old door in the high brick wall you will see, in the middle of a big garden, a fine old farmhouse. The farmhouse has many windows and tall chimneys. In the garden there are many big trees: oaks, beeches and cedars. Behind the many bushes, there is also a big pond. In the garden there are lots of paths[2] with flowers and bushes on both sides.

***

Let's open the door and follow one of the paths. Here is a path that goes to the bottom[3] of the garden. At the bottom of the garden, there is a high wall, and an old garden shed[4]. Mr Bloom the gardener keeps his fork and spade and other garden tools in the shed. And look, there at the side of the shed, in a little patch of sunshine, is the big heap of leaves that Mr Bloom collected

1 *crack* – Spalte
2 *path* – Fußweg
3 *bottom* – Ende
4 *garden shed* – Schuppen

last autumn. Quietly now. Come close[5] to the leaves and listen.

"Awhhrr," said a sleepy voice from deep in the pile of leaves[6]. "Awhhrr," and Harry Hedgehog yawned once again. "It feels a bit warmer now and I think that spring could be here," he murmured. He stretched his little back legs and his spines[7] rustled against the nest of leaves. "Mmm, I feel quite hungry after that long sleep," he said, as he yawned once again. "I must find my way out of here and have a look outside. Perhaps there is something to eat out there."

He slowly pushed his way through the pile of leaves. They had kept him warm through the cold winter. He came out of the leaves into the sunshine and sniffed the spring air with his little black nose.

"Yes," he said, "the warmer days are here at last. Now for something to eat."

---

5 *close* – nahe
6 *pile of leaves* – Laubhaufen
7 *spine* – Stachel

Just as he said that, a large animal came along the path. It was making a loud noise. "Oh dear," Harry said, "I'd forgotten about him." Harry quickly went through a hole under the old shed and watched.

***

"Scrap, come back here," cried Molly. Scrap, the black and white dog had seen something near the pile of leaves. He gave another bark and went back to his young mistress. "What did you see, Scrap?" she asked. "Was it a rat?"

"Woof," answered Scrap.

"I don't like dogs," thought Harry as he went further[8] under the floor of the shed. He watched Scrap's black nose snuffling at the pile of leaves. Then Molly called Scrap again and the dog ran back to her. Harry started looking about under the shed. Then he heard a noise in front of him and saw a pair of small red eyes looking at him. "Oh dear," he thought, "first a dog and now an unfriendly rat. Let's get out of here."

He came out from under the shed and quickly ran into the bushes at the side of the path. He knew what he was looking for and soon found a nice slug[9] eating a juicy green leaf. "That tasted good after such a long sleep," he said, "I'm going to find a few more before I go back to the nest."

---

8 *further* – weiter
9 *slug* – Nacktschnecke

Chapter 2
Harry meets Susie Squirrel

During the next days, Harry came out again for a nice meal of slugs or snails[1]. Spring was really starting now and the daffodils[2] and crocusses were beginning to send up green leaves.

Suddenly, one day, Harry felt some of the leaves around his nest move and a voice said:

"Well, Mr Bloom, the winter is over now, you can move these old leaves to the compost heap."

"Yes, Mr Stephen," answered Mr Bloom, "I'll do that tomorrow morning."

Mr Stephen was a farmer and was the owner[3] of the big house and all the fields around it.

"Oh dear," thought Harry, "I'll have to find another home before tomorrow." He waited until[4] Mr Stephen and Mr Bloom the gardener had gone off to look at the pond[5] and then came out of the nest of leaves.

"Goodbye little nest," he said, "thank you for a nice warm winter home." Then he went into the bushes that were growing along the wall of the garden.

---

1 *snail* – Schnecke (mit Haus)
2 *daffodil* – Narzisse
3 *owner* – Besitzer
4 *until* – bis
5 *pond* –Teich

A few minutes later, a grey animal landed beside him. He was very surprised[6] and rolled himself into a prickly ball. Then he heard scratching noises and he slowly unwrapped[7] himself and then looked out.

"Oh, it's you, Susie Squirrel," said Harry, "I see you are awake, too."

"Yes," she replied, "and I'm hungry. I'm looking for some beech nuts[8]. I buried them last autumn."

Harry watched as she scratched holes in the soil[9] under the bushes.

"Watch out for that dog of Molly's," he said, and started on his way again. A few minutes later, he found a small heap of old leaves under some bushes. "This will be my home for the spring and summer," he said.

---

6 *to be surprised* – überrascht sein
7 *to unwrap* – auswickeln
8 *beech nut* – Buchecker
9 *soil* – Erde

Chapter 3
The Yellow Brimstone

One day, while Harry was searching for snails among some stinging nettles[1], a beautiful yellow butterfly landed a few centimetres from his nose.

"My," he said, "you are a pretty colour. You are the same colour as the yellow spring flowers over there. What's your name?"

The butterfly flew up into the air because it was surprised when it heard Harry's voice. Then it landed near him again and replied: "Oh, hello. My name's Brenda and I'm a Yellow Brimstone." Then she said proudly, "I'm usually the first butterfly in spring. I only hatched[2] from my chrysalis[3] a few hours ago."

"Well, Brenda, watch out[4] for Molly's brother. His name is Jim, and he has a big net to catch pretty butterflies. Butterflies just like you. Last year I saw him chasing them all over the garden."

---

1 *nettles* – Brennnesseln
2 *to hatch* – ausschlüpfen
3 *chrysalis* – Puppe
4 *to watch out* – sich in Acht nehmen

Suddenly, as Harry was speaking, there was a loud shout and they heard a voice. It was Molly and she cried out: "Look, Jim, there's a yellow one by the stinging nettles."

"Quick, Brenda," said Harry, "they've seen you. Fly over the wall."

"Thanks," said Brenda as she took off and flew up and over the high wall.

"You were too slow", said Molly to her brother when they came to the stinging nettles.

"No, I wasn't," said Jim, "you frightened it by shouting."

Harry went quietly deeper into the stinging nettles. He knew the children wouldn't find him there because they didn't like the stings from nettle's leaves.

***

After a few minutes Mrs Stephen, the children's mother, came along the path and called: "Hello Molly. Hello Jim. Come and have your afternoon tea. It's sandwiches and a nice chocolate cake. But don't talk to your father about the lawn[5]."

"Why, Mum?" said Molly and Jim.

"Well, he was planning to have a party on Saturday for your birthday Molly, and he was making the lawn ready for a game of croquet[6]. He wanted to surprise you."

---

5 *lawn* – Rasen

6 *croquet* – Krocket-Spiel

Chapter 4
Harry warns Melvyn Mole

Harry waited a few minutes after they had gone and then followed them along the path. He had heard what Mrs Stephen, the farmer's wife, had said about the lawn and wanted to see it. He often walked over the lawn on his way to the back of the house. Mrs Stephen kept some chickens there and also had a big vegetable garden[1]. When he arrived at the lawn, he looked across it and then started to laugh.

"Heh, heh, heh. Old Melvin Mole has been up to his tricks again. He has made his little hills right across Mr Stephen's nice flat lawn. I must try to warn Melvyn that he'll have to watch out now for Mr Bloom's mole trap[2]". This was a nasty metal trap that Mr Bloom pushed into the ground to catch moles like Melvyn.

"I told Melvyn last year that he should be more careful where he made his mole hills. Mr Bloom will make him into a pair of moleskin trousers[3]."

Harry turned round, still laughing to himself, and went back along the path towards the nettles again.

***

1 *vegetable garden* – Gemüsegarten
2 *trap* – Falle
3 *moleskin trousers* – Hosen aus Maulwurfshaut

That evening he went back to the lawn and waited until Melvyn Mole put his long nose out of one of the mole-hills.

"Hey, Melvyn," he whispered, "it's me, Harry Hedgehog."

Harry knew that Melvyn couldn't see very far, but that his hearing was very very good. Melvyn could hear a worm[4] fall into his tunnel from five metres away.

"What's the matter, Harry?" said Melvyn in his squeaky[5] voice. So Harry told him that Mr Stephen was very angry.

"You're making hills in the middle of Mr Stephen's lovely lawn," he explained, "Mr Bloom will catch you if you don't make your hills in another place. I should leave here quickly and tunnel somewhere where he can't see you."

"Oh, dear," grumbled Melvyn, "there were such lovely juicy worms under the lawn, too. But thanks for

---

4 *worm* – Wurm
5 *squeaky* – quietschend

the tip." He came out of his hole and went over to a big flower-bed. There he quickly dug a hole with his big strong front paws[6]. In a few seconds he had gone.

"I hope he keeps going in the right direction," thought Harry. "I don't know how he can see where he is going with his bad eyes. And it must be very dark in his tunnels under all that earth[7]!"

***

The moon was bright[8] in the sky now and after Melvyn had gone, Harry walked to the vegetable garden at the back of the house. Sometimes Mrs Simon the cook put out titbits on a plate for him. She liked him in the vegetable garden because he ate the slugs. These slugs liked eating the young lettuces that Mr Bloom was growing[9].

There was nothing on the plate tonight, but he found enough slugs for a good supper. When he was full, he started to go home for a sleep under his leaves. Then he heard a "Craak Craak" from the other side of the house.

"Ah," he said to himself, "I wondered[10] when they would start their terrible noise again."

He walked slowly to the front of the house and went to the big pond. He pushed his nose through the water plants and watched. There were dozens of green frogs.

---

6 *front paws* – Vorderpfoten
7 *earth* – Erde
8 bright – hell
9 *to grow* – anbauen
10 *to wonder* – neugierig sein

Some were in the water and others were sitting on the water-lily[11] leaves.

"For such small animals they certainly make a loud noise," Harry laughed to himself.

"I'm surprised they don't explode when they blow themselves up like balloons. I won't[12] get much sleep tonight with them calling so loudly," he said to himself as he wandered[13] back to his nest under the bushes.

11 *water-lily* –Teichrose
12 *won't* – werde nicht
13 *to wander* – wandern

Chapter 5
Dragonflies and ducks

The noisy frogs kept Harry awake for several nights. But, as suddenly as they had begun, they stopped and all was quiet around the pond again. "Thank goodness for that," thought Harry as he snuffled around the edge looking for some breakfast. Suddenly a big insect with large wings hovered in front of his nose and then flew off. It came back again a few seconds later then settled on a water plant a few centimetres away from Harry's nose. He watched as the insect dipped its tail in the water.

"Hello," he said, "what are you doing?" "What all dragonflies do," replied the insect, "I'm laying[1] eggs in the water."

"That's a funny thing for a beautiful dragonfly to do. Won't they get wet?"

"Of course," laughed the insect, "before we become[2] dragon-

1 *to lay* – legen
2 *to become* – werden

flies, we have to spend a long time swimming under the water. Then, when the warm days come, we climb up a water plant and then we can fly away. Then, after a few days, we lay our eggs once more."

Just then there was a wooshing noise which frightened Harry and the dragonfly. The dragonfly flew away and Harry quickly rolled himself into a tight[3] ball. He heard two splashes[4], one after the other, and then "quack-quack, quack-quack".

"Oh, it's Micky Mallard and his wife Dolly come back again this year," he thought as he unrolled[5] himself. He watched as they swam over to the small island and climbed on it. They immediately[6] started building their old nest again. Dolly would soon lay her first eggs.

"Pity[7] they are on that island," he sighed, "because I like a nice egg now and again. It makes a change from the snails and slugs."

***

Dolly and Micky must have heard him because they started quacking and looking at him.

"I'd better leave them," he thought and quickly ran back to his nest under the bushes.

---

3 *tight* – fest
4 *splash* – Plumpser
5 *to unroll oneself* – sich ausrollen
6 *immediately* – sofort
7 *pity* – schade

Chapter 6
Harry has a lucky escape

Across the road from the big house and garden was one of Mr Stephen's fields. Harry decided[1], one evening, to have a look at the field. He had been there last year and found some tasty pheasant[2]'s eggs. Sometimes a pheasant would fly over the wall into the garden. Then Jim usually chased it with his net and it flew back to the field again. He climbed through a gap[3] at the bottom of the gate in the wall and started to cross the road. Suddenly, a fast car came round the bend[4] and blinded Harry with its headlights.

He rolled into a ball and lay still. He felt the wind from the car pass over him. The car wheels just missed

1 *to decide* – sich entschließen
2 pheasant – Fasan
3 *gap* – Lücke
4 *bend* – Kurve

his spines. He unrolled himself and shook his head. He quickly ran to the other side of the road and called out, "Road hog." Harry didn't know how lucky he had been. His sister Hattie, who had disappeared[5] last year, had been run over by a fast car.

He went through the hedge and into the field. He found that Mr Stephens had planted the field with wheat[6]. He started pushing his way through the long stalks[7]. Suddenly a small voice said:

"Hey, watch where you are going." Harry looked all around him but couldn't see anyone.

"I must have dreamed it," he thought and held a stalk with his paw. He could see a small snail on it.

***

"Stop that," said the small voice, "you'll have us down on the ground next." Harry looked up and there at the top of the stalk was a tiny mouse. It was clinging to a little nest at the top of the stalk.

"Who are you," asked Harry, "and what are you doing up there?".

"My name is Milly," said the little creature, "I'm a harvest mouse. We build our nests up here at the top[8] of the stalks."

---

5 *to disappear* – verschwinden
6 *wheat* – Weizen
7 *stalk* – Stängel
8 *at the top* – am oberen Ende

"Sorry, little mouse," said Harry, "I didn't expect[9] to see a mouse nest up in the sky. I'll be more careful next time."

And he went back out of the field to the hedge. He looked both ways. There was no car so he ran across the road as fast as he could and back under the gate to his own garden. Then he walked along the path to the pond.

---

9 *to expect* – erwarten

Chapter 7
Roddy the red fox

After he had had a good feed of slugs and snails along the edge of the pond, he walked slowly back to his nest of leaves. He had just started to have a nice sleep when there was a terrible bang from behind the house. A few minutes later there was another bang near the pond and Harry heard Mr Stephen's voice shouting. He peeped carefully[1] out of the leaves. Then a large animal crept into the bushes near him. He quickly rolled into a ball and listened.

Then he heard Mr Stephen walking along the path. Mr Bloom was with him and Harry heard Mr Bloom ask: "How many chickens did he take?"

1 *to peep carefully* – vorsichtig hervorlugen

"Only one," replied Mr Stephen, "but he killed at least four more."

"Oh, dear," thought Harry, "I'm under a bush with Roddy the red fox."

"He ran in here, somewhere," said Mr Bloom. He had a torch[2] with him. Harry could hear Roddy's heavy breathing[3]. Mr Bloom shone his torch here and there among the bushes.

***

Harry opened his eyes and looked over at Roddy. He saw that Roddy had a chicken in his mouth.

"I must get out of here," he thought, "or they'll shoot me, too." He quickly unrolled himself and rushed out of the bushes.

"There's something," shouted Mr Stephen. Mr Bloom turned the light of the torch in Harry's direction.

"No, don't shoot, Mr Stephen" he said, "it's only our old friend the hedgehog. He's harmless[4] in the garden."

With his foot, Mr Bloom pushed Harry, who had rolled into a ball again, under some bushes.

"I'll go and get Scrap from the kennel[5], he'll find that fox soon enough," he said.

As soon as the two men had turned back to get the

---

2 *torch* – Taschenlampe
3 *breathing* – Atmen
4 *harmless* – harmlos
5 *kennel* – Zwinger

dog, Harry saw Roddy creep out of the bush and run along the path. The poor chicken was still in his mouth. Then Scrap came barking and snuffling into the bushes.

"He can smell the fox," said Mr Bloom as Scrap followed the path where Roddy had gone, "we'll soon[6] have that thief[7] now."

***

"Not if I know Roddy," thought Harry as he quietly made his way home.

"Harmless am I," he laughed to himself as he got into his leaves again, "better tell that to the ducks."

---

6 *soon* – bald
7 *thief* – Dieb

Chapter 8
Harry has a chat with Billy Badger

A few nights later Harry decided he would visit Mr Stephen's small wood. It was next to the field where he had met Milly the harvest mouse. He went under the gate and ran quickly across the road. He went along the hedge and soon came to the wood. Billy the old badger lived in his hole[1] called a set in the wood. Badgers like to come out in the late evenings and Harry sometimes saw Billy outside his set. Harry liked talking to Billy. Billy knew all the gossip[2] about the animals in the wood.

***

This time Billy was there. He was snuffling about, his black and white striped face shining in the moonlight.

"Oh, hello, young Harry," he said. "I suppose[3] you've come for a chat[4]."

"Yes," replied Harry, "did you hear the loud bangs the other night? That was Mr Stephen trying to shoot Roddy the fox. He stole one of their chickens."

---

1 *hole* – Loch
2 *gossip* – Klatsch, Tratsch
3 *to suppose* – annehmen
4 *chat* – Schwätzchen

"Don't talk to me about that thief Roddy," replied Billy. "I was out and he came here with the chicken. He crept into my set to eat it. When I came home a few hours later, he had left all the feathers[5] everywhere. I had to take them out and hide[6] them."

"Yes, Mr Gould the gamekeeper[7] would think you stole it," said Harry.

"Yes," replied Billy, "he thinks it's me that chases his young partridges[8]."

Suddenly Billy looked up and sniffed the air, "I can hear someone coming through the woods at this moment," he whispered. "It could be Mr Gould the gamekeeper. Come into my set. He will have his dog

5 *feather* – Feder
6 *to hide* – verstecken
7 *gamekeeper* – Wildhüter, Jäger
8 *partridge* – Rebhuhn

with him." Billy was right. After a few minutes, a dog started snuffling at the entrance of the set.

"Come back here, Bruce," said a quiet voice, "we're not interested in old Billy Badger. Tonight we're after[9] something tastier."

***

After they had gone, Billy said, "That wasn't George the gamekeeper, it was Pete the poacher[10]. He wants to catch some of Mr Stephen's pheasants. Wait a few minutes and then run back to your garden, little Harry. It will be safer there than in these woods, tonight."

---

9 *to be after* – hinterher sein
10 *poacher* – Wilderer

Chapter 9
Harry meets a new friend

A few weeks later, Harry lay quietly in his nest under the bushes listening to the quacking of the ducks on the pond. He knew that the eggs had hatched.

"I expect Micky and Milly will soon be taking the new little ducklings for trips around the pond," he thought. "I'm glad I didn't eat any eggs. I like to see those little balls of fluff swimming on the water."

Just then he heard a rustling and snuffling noise the other side of the bushes.

"Not that dog again, I hope," he said. He pushed his nose carefully out of the leaves and suddenly he was facing[1] another little black nose like his own.

"Who are you?" he asked.

"Oh, you frightened me," said the other hedgehog. "My name is Hilary, I saw these leaves and thought it would be a good nest."

"Well, you can use it, too if you like," said Harry and made room for her.

***

---

1 *to face* – gegenübestehen

They were a very happy pair and went out hunting for tasty meals together every evening. Harry showed her the vegetable garden at the back of the house and warned her about Scrap the dog.

One warm moonlit night[2], Harry came home from hunting snails and had a big surprise. There in the nest were three little baby hedgehogs. Very soon, they too were running between the bushes in the garden. Mrs Stephen was very pleased[3] when they visited the vegetable garden. She often put out more titbits[4] for the young ones. Harry and Hilary were very proud[5] of them.

Let us go back out of the garden now and leave Harry and Hilary to look after[6] their children. They must be

---

2 *moonlit night* – Mondnacht
3 *to be pleased* – erfreut sein
4 *titbit* – Leckerbissen
5 *proud* – stolz
6 *to look after* – sich kümmern um

well fed and get nice and fat before the winter starts. Then, as the autumn leaves start to fall, they must all look for their own warm places for the cold winter months. I'm sure Mr Bloom will leave lots of piles of leaves around the garden for our little hedgehogs to find and sleep safely until it's spring again.